T0354863

A Slice of Life

A
Slice
of Life

A Poetry made by Geraldine Brooks

Geraldine Brooks

A SLICE OF LIFE
A POETRY MADE BY GERALDINE BROOKS

iUniverse books may be ordered through booksellers or by contacting:

iUniverse
1663 Liberty Drive
Bloomington, IN 47403
www.iuniverse.com
844-349-9409

ISBN: 978-1-6632-6412-1 (sc)
ISBN: 978-1-6632-6413-8 (e)

Print information available on the last page.

iUniverse rev. date: 06/21/2024

Contents

"Hollywood Lights Camera's Action"

The glamour.
The glitter.
The walks.
The movie producers.
The celebrities beautiful Tiffany and Co.
The beautiful streets cliffs. Mountains.
Diamonds beautiful clothes. Cars. Homes.
The beautiful building's Restaurants.

People.
Beautiful people.
Lights camera.
Action lets get started.
Too the good life escargo's.

Steak dinner's.
A good movie.
Sking boating walks in beautiful "parks" meeting the best of celebities.

Tour "buses".
Oh what great fun Aspen.

Italy.
Sweden.

The beautiful walk of fame the beautiful plane rides.
What beautiful people.

"Hurray."

For Hollywood.
We could go on forever.
And ever.

Oh do we love "Hollywood"

Aspen

No words for the beauty of the wilderness.
Every time you see it all you see is Americas beauty.
Its such a beautiful city as Denver being the capital of the ski lodges.

Especially Aspen is the "queen" and soul of Colorado
breath taking husbands and wives people flock here "yearly" too
feel and see the beauty of the real Colorado.

John Denver must have flown past here hundreds of times enhancing the beauty.
The ski lodges fire crackling warming the "beautiful" people
as they nestle around cups of hot chocolate marshmallows.

Beautiful blankets.
Little kids chuckling a brow enjoying this beautiful "sight"
and what a beautiful sight too see.
Lodging everything great.

Aspen.
You are so very beautiful

Miss Geraldine Brooks

The Olympics

The Olympics always fun to see swimmers skiers.
The beam walkers' winter.

Summer.
All of these events are so much fun.
Especially the winning of the gold medals.
The athletes always egar too succeed and win.

And always do the many beautiful cities that
Represent this big and beautiful event.
No words for the talent or the shows.

Just plain fun.
And very beautiful people.
The marathon runners.
Boy what speed.
Any and everything that you see is so much fun.
Do we love the Olympics?

Miss Geraldine Brooks

The New Years Eve
Ball Dropping

Beautiful.

Classy.

Traditional who ever thought of this event
what a very brillant and beautiful person.

When it falls it looks like so much class
and the "beautiful" dressed people from all over the world
enjoying the worlds celebration of beauty and class.

And fun.
So special.
And so beautiful.

There are no words for this beautiful event of people
just plain class and "beauty."
The Corona virus threatened this beautiful event,
but not for long.

It was back up like everything else.
And back too life.
This is one of the most "beautifulest" events ever in the "world."
And what a great and powerful city, New York.

Live on.
New Years ball dropping

                    Miss Brooks

"The Trade Center Collapse"

One two three four.
And they all came down.
Building's "falling" stone everywhere.

Everywhere.
You turned "concrete" concrete was the world turning too
"concrete" did we get too do pottery.

"Sculptur" or "molding"
what was it "concrete" rain concrete lunch
"the" American journalism has finally be "falleen" work
and the journalism history.

As great as McVeigh and the "Unibomber"
a classic what did you learn from it.
The American terrosits that was never caught.
You were suppose too have learned something from that.
The teaching was stop begging if you go too Chicago.

You will see the two cousins standing side by side beautiful building's.
Representing the two towers that we're tore down by the "American"
Some of the greatest pieces of work ever
lived of a terrorists there has been many
but this act was "spontaneous" "done" so very "perfect."

Neatly.
It was time for a teaching trough death
for this city full of "snitches" fake people.
Well you have "them" all over the world.

"Scary."

"Miss Brooks"

Nevada Las Vegas

Las Vegas
A very beautiful city full of beautiful lights.

Hotels casinos.
Gorgeous the showgirls the food "delicious."
The "fun" non-stopping.

The tours.
Buses of people coming from everywhere too
Look at the beautiful hotels.
The Hilton. MGM Grand.

The Win.
The fun.
Nonstop.
Vegas.
The beautiful Las Vegas.
Even after "the" massacre.
Even after spontounsley.
Still standing.
The beautiful Las Vegas.
Glamour class.
Let's go "to the beautiful Las" Vegas.

Miss Geraldine Brooks

India

A very beautiful country.
Coal is how they make a "living."
And get rich mostly.
"Coal" they have tons of coal "mines."

And raid.
The "Egyptian."
"Tombs," but mostly coal Pakastian.
One of the most beautifulest ones.

The beautiful clothes hats "gowns."
They lost a lot too.
And some of those people do not want.
You "wearing" their "clothes."
Sick you should be happy.
Some one likes your culture too wear.

Your "clothes."
Some of the women are not that "attractive."
The building's and the "events" very "beautiful."
China Japan "Jupiter" all of those "countries"
have very beautiful "celebrations"
and "events" try them

Miss Brooks

"Madison"

Colleges Art Cold but very "historical" and great.
The schools outstanding.
The teachers are so "brilliant."
In addition, classy very "brilliant" and care.
The campuses "breath" taking.

Theatre.
Art.
The restaurants.

Beautiful.
And very "tasty" the building,
Very historical and "educated".
So very "feelings".

I did 2 yrs. there.
The schools make you feel so very like "someone."

The classrooms.
Beautiful chairs.
Letting you know that you are some one.
In addition, anything that sat there turned out to be someone.

Nurses.
Presidents.
"Doctors" Lawyers.
The college "bars."
Boy do I love Madison.

"Miss Brooks"

"Florida"

A very beautiful content just full of very selfish people.
Beautiful homes "beaches" "restaurants" parks ect.

Night clubs.
"Just" selfish people.
The homes awesome.
The "state" reminds you of it's like being stranded on a beautiful island.

And then you say America.
It truly shows how beautiful America is.
Tampa Miami Fort Meyers.
Palm Beach. Palm "Spring's" Bonita Spring's just gorgeouse.
The homes look "like" homes that are on a beautiful "island."
"Florida" the aligators the "beautiful" "animals" are so very awsome.

Beautiful.
The manatees.
The cute "little" geico's that run around.
Delicious food.
Events.
No words for the never-ending "fun."
So come join in the "festivies" and fun

Miss Brooks

"The Little Mouse Who Came"

Hi I am Mandy where's the cheese.
No mouse traps.
I grabbed a crumb.
"Peeked."
Looked.
No "cheese".
I need anything.
Cheese.
Crumbs.
Death is "near."
Aah. The trap.
It's over.
Kids aah.
We're "gone."
It's over the sunlight the moon.
The sewers.
We hide in aah.
No more crumbs.
No more sewers to hide in.
Aah here "comes," the poison troops.
Let's go aah.
Too late.

"That was the mouse who came"

Miss Brooks

"The Beautiful Hells Angels"

Motorcycles shining so bright clean high "spirited.
Americans proud of their country.
And how they represent it yeah - yeah.

Riding high.
Clean.
Leather vest showing.
Class decencee and respect for one's self.
The beautiful Hells Angels.
No drugs can stop the respect or lies of filth
That sick people bring always a wont to be.

This ant won't to be this is real human love country
and love for government.
Life respect it and keep your sick thoughts
and comments to yourself.
And watch.
And respect the life and "times,"
of the "angel" dead and alive.
And ride.

Geraldine Brooks

"The Capital Hill Attack"

It was so sudden.
A mob of people "stormed" into the capital building to attack the people there.
The stimulius.

Check.
The last one was the reason not Trump.
News people lie especially when they are afraid of something.
Fear bring's "lies".
It was a beautiful piece of history.

"Truithful" justice great and beautiful work for mankind.
Not a one schould have went to jail for your slow work.
When it comes too beautiful nice people
who live to make the world a better place,
you be on time.

                    "Miss Geraldine Brooks"

"Death"

Death to me from viosoliging is a "warm" feeling beautiful.
A welcome from "life" that a break.
Everyone is waiting for but "right" everyone
knows how they're suppose too go.
Not "murder" stick up.
"Drive bys" "suicides" car accidents
some people live decently until death.
And that's how they go out.
"Decently" "like" how they lived.
When I think of it I see and feel a beautiful
"feeling" like a dose of "vicodine" or a painkiller pill.
And you go too sleep and never wake up by life
its over work and play.
Time to rest it's about time "peace" at last
no more bull shit when there was suppose too be peace.
Peace at last I've lived missed nothing but fucking you up.
Mostly for being worsome and "ungrateful."
So go and be worthy and grateful.
Instead of an "asshole" somebody who don't care about nothing but self.
Make this world a better place to live in.

Until your "beautiful" death

Miss Brooks

"The Beautiful"
"Snake"

My eyes are so very gorgeous.
Hated by many.
I won't bother you if you've done "nothing."
How did God make me "without" dying.
The hands ever glear.
Water without "dying" or "drowning" ever glee again.
Meaning flesh that I didn't "desenerate" fire
and didn't burn humans that "exists" water falls "beautiful" word.
Wow money for "support" him
for whatever that you may need if he's there for you.
What a "beautiful "reptile" for a female.
Too patter themselves after they never do I "slither."
I crawl "beautifully" explore.
Looking for evil "doers."
Let me "catch" you when I'm angry.

The Spider

I love spinning webs the "spider" long legs beautiful face,
eyes that tell the "story" of the dangerouse "poisoning's"
that flow through the beautiful body of the "spider."
I crawl in spaces that no "one" can see holes.

Mostly are my "hiding" "places"
Anywhere you see a web I'm there. I love "spinning" webs.
My "specialty" oh the webs look so very "nice"
do I love too spin. My homes alway's look "like" a spinning wheel.
So neatly done

Aah. I'm "being" torn down why did I have to come down.
Ooh. Well if "that's" how you feel aah life goes no "more."
I guess it's time to be "desengrated" gone "forever."
No more aah.

The beautiful spider

Miss "Brooks"

Queen Elizabeth
the Royalty
the beautiful queen

The funeral no words. The beautiful funeral posession carrying the preciouse body of some one so very great. It seemed like eternity before it was over 10 day's of nothing but absolute beauty. Well we didn't know she loved are cared for beauty. Such as trees nature. Peroid. What queen. Loves nature. Besides Snow White and the Seven Dwarfs. This beautiful soul did. 72 yrs hard yrs of beautiful peaceful work and got around. So very beautifully even after the death of her daughter in law Diana. Camille was the life and strength as the fate of "London" was at hand. For certain the fate of London needed it's future queen, as life is not forever. Not even for the truithful queen. London arrived. Everything was Ok.

The crown looked like she was still wearing it as it stood among the British soldiers. So historically it reminded you of a beautiful person. The one who wore it so very beautifully and well buried by King "Arthur" and the king. What a beautiful piece of history especially in pitcures. Megan the Dutchess.

Phillip and the beautiful daughter Charles Camille. All the beautiful family was there. The world will alway's love the thoughtful beautiful soul. God made who for 90 yrs brought so much peace love. No words like God for such a beautiful "lady." A woman of God. Her country dignified there is no words for such a beautiful soul, laid to rest with all the historical figures. Laid too rest my dear.

Alias at rest the crown the thorne is at its best.

"Miss Brooks"

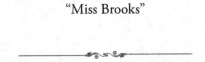

The sick people of society who live off "lust" and "greed"

Did you know that there are sick humans who live daily off "sex" and love it? I guess it's another way to escape their everyday blues of thing's that they've done "like" AIDS or maybe they just "like" treating themselves to something, amid all of their problems like having a nasty woman for a "girlfriend" or not helping you because they don't like something about themselves. Ok change it sex is not going to make you feel better.

Change will and go one and continue to live. Stop marrying people to destroy you. You are worth your life. You go and get someone who suppose too love and help.

"The Sick Male"

Always walking by itself not knowing when somebodies going to cave his head for being so filthy. Acting like someone won'ts him all the time "afraid" of being "attacked" by anybody for being so filthy. Get a job you lazy bum. And go on and take that ass whipping nasty "bitch."

Probably a'nt got 5 dollars. Shame ugly bitch and the bitch that he trying to be with is too both of you scary "bitches" get the fuck outta here before you get your ass whipped.

Filthy Bitches

Miss Brooks

The World

"Did" you know that the world is people and that they are very smart "especially" the ones with "money" and you have too be. There is a such thing as laziness which leads to begging. Stealing stealing. Can also be a need like "hunger bills" ect you see all kind of people in the world. "Lazy "smart" stupid". "Dumb" wise" successful. No money. They call this poverty. They "live pretty" well. It all depends on the person and who it is. The world has so many kinds black white Asian Greek Jamacian African lation. There are ove 200 different cultures in the world today. Wis and very smart nothing is going past them. Never. They look and make decisions. Just hope if you are in need that you were in the giving space or maybe you didn't need anything never. And had it already or was going too get it yourself "Congrulations" its "good" to put your self first depend on no one not even "God." You are your best "everything" friend. Everything mama daddy. You are your best everything.

So live it. And let no one tell you different and your "cash" it is everything its no telling where you may wand up at this great big ole word. You and the cash will be Ok until your "departure" so when you get ready too depart you will be Ok. And keep until departure. Keep the golddiggers out "lust greed" the two most "busiest" words that keep you working like a dog. "Broke" unless you like doggings another word for floogings. The human body can take so much. Are you iron or "steele" that's why they have "robots" so when the human body get's tired they take over. They have over 12 million working right now write a good poem or book. When you get "bored" there is no such thing as loneliness. It's a hustling word to make money like "sex" loneliness and sex are two of the main words that het quick cash not "baby." Do you know how many people give them selves to these words and go broke some even "death" so stay away from people who use these words too "survive" with the walks "hair" hats. Clothes. A conversation. A touch. A smile which is alway's ugly. It all depends on the "face" unless you won't this and live. Some will even destroy you. Male-female they be tired. They never wanted you only what you had. It's time too go. So they kill you. They feel like they are doing them selves a favor. And the world you were suppose to had left or never met this "monster." Why would you treat your self to death instead of "life" what could be effecting you like that most couples know their "fate" do you like destroying your self. You hate your self that bad. What did you do. Change and live or go one. And be self destruct. That's not love that's "stupidy" be by yourself. There are nice people. Find them or be by your self or socialize life's great. Find the right person. If you choose too date not "destruction"

Miss Brooks

"The Harley "Davidson"

One of the most "beautifulest" bikes ever made. You cannot even describe the beauty of the "bike" its so beautiful there are so many. The designer. Rest in peace. Fate must have known it was going too be a winner. As the designer upon the arrival of the beautiful object was laid too rest but never the beautiful object he "displayed" which "has won" hearts of "billions" with the beautiful design of the "Harley." There are no words for the beauty of the "bike." Like God, it's just a "beautiful" object that the world loves going "hurray, hurray" too and ah oh. How beautiful and yes. What a beauty. No words for the great designer or "bike" just a beauty and the designer. Another great "designer" who was one of the best

"Harley live on."
You're "the greatest"

Miss Geraldine Brooks

Life "Succeed" Live Be Happy

To live your beautiful life means being happy letting no body getting you down with their sick lies. Don't listen. Ignore and laugh at these sick people. You owe nothing to no one but god. And not even him if you choose not too. Live succeed. Stay away from sick fearful living people. You won't gain nothing but hatred stay yourself.

Laugh at these sick dumb ass people if you have an idea. Some one is waiting too help you. It might not be who you want but some one will be there. Follow your mind. Don't listen never to no dummy. You will learn or earn nothing only "sickness" and madness. They know they are losers.

Life

What happened?
It use too be so very giving.
No one never slept on the streets or went without like they are doing now.
What happened.
I think that it was the "ass" "epemidic people got more into this.
That's where a lot of it went well pedophiles never have nothing too offer.
And no one won'ts nothing.
If you don't won't too give it they go on
and get it themselves until their death so enjoy your life wealth.
Whatever you won't to do.
Do it.
It's your life live on.
No one's mad.
They're happy for you.
Someone will be there.
You know that that's why you did that so have fun.
Beautiful word.

Miss Brooks

43

Business the Business World

I did not know that it was that bad until I lived it.

You can have lay overs at bus stations and wand up sleeping outside of the bus station waiting on the bus. Around another building too block the wind. I did not know that this was part of the business world. People knowing you're going to accomplish your dreams won't help. Support the cause and need the money. There are some real "dummies" in the world. How do you turn down something that you're going too need. That's stupidy. Running out of money having too stay in towns or places waiting on money that ran out. You tell yourself I will succeed. That bills. Your business still goes on as people know how people and the world is. Not everyone there are still millions of good people and they die like this.

You can run into all kinds of money in your life and can not claim it. It's true that all money is not good money. It's so depressing how you needed it. And you had too pass it by that's why so many go on and get their own. And why it takes so long too "succeed" sick. Still there are bills and you are going too pay them. These are thing's you need too know. So go on and live but remember these thing's

So live

Miss Geraldine Brooks

Summer Fun

Basketball, Barbeques "picnics."
Summer Camps "Tanning" swimming.
Barbeque "ribs" hotdogs and they really do taste good.
At summer time.
Summer fun.
Yeah.
Shorts feets out "beaches" job "corps" fast "cars"
the sun "shining" people moving about.
Traveling as any other day.
Like summer winter spring "and" fall."
Life goes on.
I'm so happy to feel better.
Instead of the cold brutal winter icy storms.
Killing you making you sick.
Without heat.
Heartless.
Imagine a decent human who's given so much.
All of a sudden is frozen too die
and you will thousands have thank the world for summer

Miss Brooks

The Justice "that Justicefies"

The justice that justifies is people
who let you know that there is justice
for anything that some of these sick minded people "have" with them.

Isn't it beautiful too know that every
and any thing is "justified" God made it like that.
Why can't you accept it.
You're beaten at your own "selfishness" huh.
Change that's the only way out, you'll live so beautifully.
Anything is justified, "proudly" and decently.
Change or face the "justice system" "world."

"Miss Brooks"

Winter

Deadly anywhere in the world.
You could even loose your life. The brutal winters.
So prepare your selves summer.

Winter spring and fall for the brutal winters. World wide. How in the hell have humans managed too live to millions and twenty three yrs. in these harsh winters. Chicago New York Colorado. How did you ever survive. I guess "surviving" and being "determined" to do so can you imagine the hard ship burning flesh of icey winds. Good beautiful people. Done absolutely nothing that never "deserved" this type of weather in stage "coaches" on horses.

Even the horses the beautiful animals dying from the freezing cold. Why would you invent a world too do such "harsh" treatment to man kind and the beautiful animals. Why. Why. Would you destroying all your creations.

Things that you're suppose too love.

What type of person is this. Some one jealouse of his own "creations." That's what that is for two million twenty three yrs. My God. Why would you make something and you knew what was going to be but you made it anyway.

Is this some type of freak. If you make something especially if it came from your body and you love your self. You love it also not kill it and it's done absolutely nothing.

This makes no sense. I wouldn't and would not have made nothing to make me look bad or ask these type of "questions."

You don't question something that you love nor destroy it unless it becomes fatal. And then you don't meet it.

No answers still. We know with out your answers. No problem can be solved.

Remember especially in life the "brutal" winters

Miss Brooks

"The Police Department"
of today
Nation Wide

———————

The cops.
The police department of today.
They don't be playing catching cases.

Left and right.
Bring it on. They're still the same just especially ever more.
Strict with fake riots going on.
Bullshit they are still then same police department faithful. Stop.
Disrespecting your help and respect "it"
the police departments of the "world."

Miss Brooks

———————

"The Pretty Zebra"

The beautiful zebra.
So many beautiful stripes.
Standing so proudly and beautiful.
The stripes look like before Keebler.
Cookies just any kind of delicious ice cream.
A very pretty animal.
Always so quiet as it is the baby of the wilderness.
One of the "prettiest" animals the woods have too offer.
And the forest the beautiful "zebra."
Besides the peacock and as you know that she is the queen of the birds.
Where did the creator get these "beautiful" creatures from. With in his head
he only knows the beautiful animals. So many. As the beautiful zebra.

Miss Brooks

Me and "Jennie"

Hey Jennie what's going on nothing. Meet me at Starbuck. We'll go and drink coffee. And look at all the city slickers yeah that be in the city.

What are you doing tomorrow reading, mountain climbing, jogging."

I've got to "finish" these 4 yrs. So I can get this job. How many yrs. do you "have" left.

2. Yale is a very "beautiful" school yes it is. How many more do you have left.

2. Marketing and these test's get "harder" and "harder." Hang in there you won't regret it. Boston really is a very beautiful state. Its just so "cold." I know. So what do you do there games "parities" snow sledging.

Work. Enjoy the beautiful festistivies.

"Arting museums" shopping. What do you do there in "Manhattan." Work shop. Pay bills I will be down too see you next week. Ok. There are some empty dress shops in New York you won't too go in business. Sure. More money for the future how much is the rent eight hundred. Can you believe that. Yeah people need money. So the price comes down. They know there's cheaper. How's Calif. Ok. I'm visiting there next week. How's Howard. Fine tell him hi. And I miss and love "him" Jennie what are you doing today. Same as every. Jennie do you remember when we went too medevil times how much fun we had yes. We are going to Madrid next. How are your nails. Fine. Is Cindy still in "Indiana" yes, doing just fine. Tomorrow I'm going up there to do some business tell Harold hi. When are we going too Vegas again. Soon. They have discounts on "tickets." I went too the store yesterday. And had a ball "flowers" for spring seeds "Garden hats" accessories. Thing's like warter hoses. Lights for the lawn just a "host" of gardening equipment. Water "hoses" "bird seeds" bird baths just a host of beautiful "thing's" spring is around the corner. Bird baths "fences" just a host of house care "things." And spring is "fun" cleaning so Sarda went on too "Rome." Huh. Yeah. So Jennie we'll be going too Columbus next week. Ok. I wish we had paning license. We could also go to Arizonia and pan for "cold." What fun "huh"

Yeah. Bill Johnsons barbque restaurant is still there. They have very good "barbque" there I "hear" the "pottery" and molding in Cincinati is his. Oh well did Judy ever start "pottery" "classes." Yes she did. And made 6 pots. Ok then. We'll probally go and explore Florida this year. Look at some of the "manantees," and the beautiful "beaches" Marco "island" Clearwater Daytona Beach Miami

Dub. Yeah. Were going to explore some of their beaches especially in the Mediterean Sea those beaches over there are beautiful also. I'm alway's looking at them on the web.

Let's not forget the Bahamas breath taking and paradise

My God girl. We have got too save this "money." What are you cooking for "dinner" just macaroni and cheese and a few "anchioves" "tray's" with a few "siskabobs." Some grilled onions and white wine. Bartle and "James." We have got too visit those vin yards and the "queens" grave the "yards" also I've got too start planning for vacationing. I think this year. We'll also visit the Chinese "Bridge" the glass one. I'm so "excited"

Well we have so much too do.

The "Cities of the World and Centuries Ago

The cities of the world are so very beautiful "Chicago" New York.

Germany Paris. Not to "mention" centuries "ago" especially the ones built in the mountains. No words for the "beautiful" lives that lived and "died" there, the mountain parties. The beautiful clothes. Jewelery. Hand made Gothan was the prettiest. Jericho one of the "prettiest" even the ones God destroyed centuries ago "Babylon" was the "greatest" and Sodom and "Gomorrah" very powerful and glitter and "glamorouse" like New York or "Vegas" two of the most powerfulest ones of "today." LA also. The rest falls in line and are "powerful" rich. Not also speaking of the farming "cities" breath taking.

There are no words for how clean and "powerful" they are. The beautiful "Cities "of the" "world."

"The Children the Plane and Mom the Flowers"

Ma ma. Where do all of the pretty flowers come from. God. Mom "replied" look how they bloosom. And oh they smell ever so wonderful look at how the "lillies" grow. The plane mom. Look how beautiful look at how it glides say's mom. Look over there. "Tulips." They are ever so beautiful. The dafoldils. What a beautiful. God making such beautiful thing's. As the beautiful flower. And powerful "planes" and a beautiful mom. Aren't we so lucky kids. "Yes" replied the "children." Mom can we look at more flowers. Of "course" the dandolines show how very much God loves you did. You know that. Yeah mom. How about the tulips again.

Lovely and beautiful roses. Oh the Iris's just takes you away. The Carnations breath taking.

The orchids. Minds of their own. The Fresia. Lovely and the hyncinth. Very "historical" don't ever speak of the African "Daisy." A tradition and the achiller. Desert eve. Ever so beautiful the deep rose I just love them. They are so very beautiful especially in wedding's & proms. Funerals. Not speaking of the African Lily. No words. Look kids at the bonsai and the dasies. Oh my God they always smells like fresh earth. The world look at your favorite one Ellie Jasmine. The lotus "disappears." Every spring and return. Every 3 yrs. lets go over by the play ground none. Mom no more flowers. What do we do now. Well go and bake cookies and have milk and later go and walk Harold the family dog tomorrow

Well go to the museum and look at "King" Tut. Did you know that he came all the way from Egypt and was a real "king." Yes. We'll learn more tomorrow "dinner" time. Kids yeah. What's for dinner "mom" hot dogs and french fries. Yeah. After dinner mom can we play catch. Yes but not in the street's kids and watch out for the cars. Shower's are at 8:00 be on time Ok mom. Let's go down by the river and look at the crocodiles and play with the flowers. Ok. Lets go look at Jill how did she learn how too ride her bike. So good.

Her mom took time out too help. Don't forget the "skate board." And the rocks for the "crocodiles." Look at that one hugh just act like you don't see it and up and scram. Mom can we have snacks.

2 cookie's each and one glass of lemonade only. Ok mom. Dinner was great. I love grilled hot dog's. And the "french fries" yeah. Can we have more mom. No you've had enough.

Mom Jenny didn't do the "dishes"

Jenny get up and do the "dishes"

Or no bike riding or dessert. Ok mom. Mom where are my gym "shoes." And my kite oh. I see them mom. What's for dinner Mom "lasagna." Yeah. I love your "lasagna" and all the beautiful "casseroles" that you fix. Especially the "banana" nut "bread" and the lemonade. Mom so great. Ok kids nap time. Sesame Street when you a wake or "Star Trek" alright mom. Zzzzzzz. Mom were ready for dinner. Can we go to the park and buy lemonade and cookies tomorrow.

Yes after I check your home work. And out of those school clothes. The lemonade was deliciouse mom and the cookies. They were great.

Especially the chocolate chip cookies my teacher is so nice mom I date her board every morning. She's pregnant. Oh well. So much for kids for kids sake. We're going on a news paper route Monday. Yeah. I get too deliver "papers" yeah mom. We've got too get our routes. "Ready." Sarah which ones do you won't the school ones. I love watching the little kids they are so very "funny." So will you take Sun Bird up too Halston. And well meet you upon Brewery. Then well go and have pizza.

Yeah. This pizza is so good mom full of "anchioves" and "cheese" and mushrooms they are so deliciouse, the "mushrooms" delicouse. Cheese next mom, can we have extra "anchoives."

Yea. Were going too the Cubs game after we leave here. Yeah "again" Monday after school can we go to boy's and girls also mom. Yeah after home work. Mom are we going too basket ball Thursday.

Why of course Ok mom we love you mom. You're the "greatest" mom. I know, I know. Bed "time" "oh" mom where's my teddy bear Mom.

In the corner.

Hi Teddy hi mom can Cassie come to the park with us. Yeah. And Roger. Roger is so ambicitious and fun.

Well bring along sandwiches and have a small "picnic" yeah. Easter's coming. Look at the beautiful basket's. And the Easter egg hunt's what about the chocolate "bunnies" they are so "good" mom

What taste "buds" you have my "dears" mom look at the "sunset" it's beautiful. Let's take a "pitcure" yeah.

No boat rides mom yea come on guys. "Yea" the lemonade sheds are up mom - oh great. And fresh. Where are the "hog dog's" and peanuts

Mom over there let's go and grab some
Mom Ok slow down.
Cassie come on.
The hot dog's relish mustard great. Did dad show up. Yes. And had 2.

Well. Home wood bound we had lot's of fun tomorrow swimming "summer "fun." Yeah. Rope jumping crocodile "spetting's" so much fun mom. Life is "exciting" and fun. Let's go horse back riding yeah.

Water throwing, cake eating hot dog's also. Remember the last one mom. I won yes you did. 50 bucks.

Life is fun

Mom what's going on tomorrow. Museum swimming. Boys and girls club. So be ready. And act Ok. Your day is going to be so beautiful. And then "Universal" "Studios" yeah mom. Home work. Let's get "busy." Ok mom. Church Sunday. And at our best also, as alway's. Yeah. Mom. Your the best. Is every one ready too pick all the beautiful preciouse flowers "bloosming" yea we are. Let's go mom. Sandy. "Yeah." Mom why do we have too go to bed so early. School. Arts and Crafts. Yoga. Science, there are now dinasaures at the museum. So nightie night "kids." Good morning kids lets go look at the gorillas. Mom and the monkeys, they are so so very funny Mom.

Could we have ice cream now mom. Yes. Look at all the flavors. Mom. I wont vanilla what about you "Sandy." Fudge is Ok. I'll take strawberry. This ice cream is so very "deliciouse," mom the clown. Those peanuts smell. So very good. "Mmm" lets get some cotton candy. Also mom. Museum time kids let's go. "Yeah." Look at King Tut. So beautiful. You can tell when he ruled he was a mighty king. Look at the beautiful gold. The flowers also mom. Yes the tulips were "different" the daffolilds. Also mom. What beautiful "roses." Yes they are. Tomorrow mom can we go to the zoo. Yeah. If you are good kids. Yeah. There's Dad. Hi dad. How was work. Fine kids. How was exploring. Fun and we even "saw King "Tut" tomorrow dad we get to go and look at the giraffs and zebra's. I hope we see a "peacock." Me to. Up kids zoo time yeah. Were packing a lunch "today." Apples peanut butter. Sandwiches with chocolate chip "cookies" and strawberry. Kool-aide yeah. Mom can we bring Jan. Sure if her mom say it's Ok. And spend the night. And have a pillow fight. I guess so, and we're off. Yeah. Sandy slow down. Look a giraffee a funny monkey. "Ha ha" look how funny. Mom he is a laugh. Well buy him some peanuts. Why do they eat so fast mom. Hungry.

I imagine they are funny halariouse lets go and look at the dandlions.

They are very beautiful here also kids, the beautiful birds. Look there's your "peacock." Look at the beautiful wing's. The very proud walk. What a "beautiful" bird. Let's go and feed the "ducks" mom. Look there's dozen's of them mom. Out by the stream. Look. Watch them fly. The pelicans are the most "prettiest" ones. Let's go and look at the squirrells and the racoons. There's some over there. Look at how they look when they run. Mom, I know they're so very funny. Short leg's. Fat. Little "scurry" bodies. How funny. Ha ha. Looking for today's food. Funny little "thing's" lets take a look at the hugh elephants. What weight and look at those "gigantic" feets mom the funny monkey's again "ha ha" lets go for cotton candy again. Mom Ok one last time. Because you did eat all your "dinner." And all of it. Well get some tomorrow Magic Kingdom. Yeah yeah. Mom. What about Adventure World. That's next. And then medevil" times "Yeah mom" yeah. Mom thank you

You're welcome son.

Miss Brooks

The children the plane "the flowers" and mom.

———————⟨⟩———————

Printed in the United States
by Baker & Taylor Publisher Services

Printed in the United States·
by Baker & Taylor Publisher Services